FOTHERINGHAY
AND OTHER POEMS

Also by John Greening

Westerners *(Hippopotamus Press)*

The Tutankhamun Variations*(Bloodaxe)*

John Greening

FOTHERINGHAY
and other poems

" Home is where one starts from "

T. S. Eliot

John Greening

May 1995

Stonely

Rockingham Press

Published in 1995
by
The Rockingham Press
11 Musley Lane,
Ware, Herts
SG12 7EN

British Library Cataloguing-in-Publication Data

A catalogue record for this book
is available from the British Library

ISBN 1 873468 30 X

Printed in Great Britain
by Bemrose Shafron (Printers) Ltd,
Chester

Printed on Recycled Paper

Eastern Arts
Board Funded

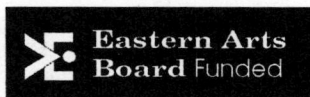

For Stephen and Elizabeth Hanvey

The loss of imperial power, the failure of
economic nerve, the diminished influence of
Britain inside Europe, all this has led to a new
sense of the shires, a new valuing of the native
English experience.

Seamus Heaney, *Englands of the Mind*

Acknowledgements

Acknowledgements are due to the editors of the following publications, in which some of these poems first appeared:

Acumen, Cumberland Poetry Review (USA), Encounter, "If you came this way: a Kimbolton Miscellany", The Independent, The New Welsh Review, Oasis, The Observer, Outposts, Oxford Poetry, Poetry Durham, Poetry Review, Poetry Wales, Quartz, The Rialto, The Spectator, Spokes and *Swansea Review.*

Huntingdonshire Eclogues have appeared in many of the above, and a selection was featured in the June 1990 edition of The Washington Times magazine *The World and I*, with accompanying illustrations by Mark Bennett.

Fotheringhay was winner of a Duncan Lawrie prize in the 1989 Arvon Poetry Competition and appeared in the prizewinners' anthology.

Katie in a Prospect of D.C. was selected by William Scammell for the Poetry Book Society Anthology 3 (Hutchinson).

Seven Sea Interludes was included in "Reflecting Families", published in 1995 by BBC Education to mark the U.N. Year of the Family.

The translation of *Autumn Manoeuvres* by Ingeborg Bachmann is included by permission of Dr. Heinz Bachmann, and the original poem in German is published by Piper Verlag, Munich.

Contents

Fotheringhay

*... the one who has placed his faith in the archetype
follows the tracks of life and lives right into his death.*

Jung

*While with an eye made quiet by the power
Of harmony and the deep power of joy,
We see into the life of things.*

Wordsworth

Fotheringhay

Fragments of what England
used to be, tucked
in corners of September:

a park, with its oaks
like a dining-room in
a stately home, thrown

open to the public, but
cordoned to keep the sheep
and their deep-pile

instincts, their appetites,
their Sunday cries of
ah! and ah! from coming

to the table. Turf
reseeded, so we may
browse where we belong.

*

Who keeps doves now? In
Eaglethorpe — where a girl,
out jogging, flusters

past me into the woods — is
a perfect dovecote. Not
just for good luck, but

to feed the golden manners
of the Lord in his great eyrie;
squabs, white as her breath-

lessness, feel his knife
pierce them to the board,
know his hidden talons.

                    *

Sheep rise, and there is a
ripple across the sky, as if
the master of its domain

with his four-wheel drive
had printed a snake-back
cirrus track, and then appeared,

making his broadcast, hands
in a nitrates bag, redeployed,
bright yellow, full of the day.

                    *

Past preaching doves, towards
a steady tolling bell,
calling the congregations

that are gone. A water-
meadow comes to feel
precious on such a morning.

A man could be a divining Y
held by the earth, and I
a jay-walker between spires.

*

The way is not direct
to that eight-sided crown,
but through a web, a zig-

zag of scaffolded planking
across the dry ducts of
a flood-plain that knows only

guttural until February.
A sluice-gate hangs like
a guillotine. Poplars press

to watch the matronym on a
pleasure craft descend into
the cold print of a lock.

*

The weir race holds forth
through all mere prattling
and there is no barrier

to stop a child falling.
No Fishing, the sign says,
but the footpath casts

towards brown eddies where
these meadows end and the church
vane is a spinning lure.

*

A lantern tower to guide
huntsmen home through
Rockingham forest, which no

visitor finds, except in
his mind, meandering
between bare fields towards

where the boar first
charged, and the red
deer lay down her false

antlers. A man in shirt-
sleeves, a camera slung
around him, leaps a stile.

The light is perfect for
a photograph of the
castle that is not there.

*

Soliloquize — don't
hurry along this green
lane, there is too much

history to be plotted.
This does not feel like
paths you have walked

on other Sundays, nor is it
because you are escaping
tensions at home, your new-

born nephew in the house,
his birthday forever
September; no, it is

the enormity of this small
hamlet you have so long
procrastinated in reaching.

*

How our own expectations
surprise us: the mound
where I had imagined

I would imagine Mary
Queen of Scots' last
toss of the head and

thread of Latin, Richard
the Third's first loss and
Yorkish howl, is today

common ground, a flag
with 'Caravan Club'
jauntily planted on the site

of the block, and a tartaned
weekender boorishly
munching bacon in the sun.

*

Overlooking a smell of
black plasticky hay
and molasses, in a loop

of the Nene, the motte
seethes like a forgotten
corpse. September's end,

and hotter than it should be,
as if the world were just
beginning to sweat at

some of the past wrongs
only now it's old enough
to feel and regret.

           *

Twin toddlers slide
down the path from
the keep; a man

and a woman restrain
an Alsatian. I inspect
two plaques on a fence

interning one fragment
of a refuge. The river
curves irretrievably.

           *

Nowhere to sit without
getting pricked or stung
to watch a power-

cruiser pass, or listen
to that robin try
to voice past freezings.

*

No day is adequate,
no life, to take in
what this hand's-breadth

offers up: but only to sit
like a stylite on one
high moment, is as much

profundity as a Sunday
in a working week
will allow: or the rev-

rev of a congregation
reversing past holes
in the sky; or the boring

pneumatic noises
people make — civil
teachers and engineers.

*

The church has a sign
on the door warning me
no valuables are inside.

Instead, everything is
out for harvest: a glazed
plait on the altar; pears,

pumpkins, marrows, eggs;
love-apples great and small;
along with the jars of

yellow pickly heat and rape-
flower honey... No valuables.
All is empty, secure.

                    *

Fotheringhay brings
home to me these natural
thoughts from the richest

soils of England. One
native pine and a hump
of briar are the last

flickerings of sleeping
booty; now autumn is
no longer rusty witchlocks,

but sun kisses earth from
open skies where hair
rises a manchet white.

                    *

The plea a village pond
makes when it's frozen
and a beer-can strikes,

the sound of everyday
returning, the freezing-
over of whatever warm

song came streaming today:
those trusty paratroopers
up in the trees palisading

the church — the rooks — pick
at Midland clay as if they
hoped to resurrect a forest.

*

A parachutist has been
released from a small
private cross, to become

micropolyphony: a whelk,
a periwinkle, in the blue
Sunday tides; it drifts

his/her hazy way down
with another and now
others like seeds from some

vanished theme; which yet soars
over the church, a falcon
freed of its fetterlock.

*

Days like this are not
given for nothing: they are
to highlight the new

haws formed in the hedges;
to focus a three-months
blur in the sky on

what matters: to teach us
to distinguish between the
grey rippling of the ash

and the torrential log-jam
of wedges in an oak. It is
to make us notice that

motionless white-tailed wind-
pump; and look up to
the hum of aerobatics.

*

Days like this are of a
glass that you can look
through and see other days.

* * *

September 1989

20

Autumn Manoeuvres

after Ingeborg Bachmann

That's all in the past, is what I don't say.
We are lying again, wallets full of summer's
Worthless notes, on chaff of derision, enduring
Time's autumn manoeuvres. And no flight-path
South with the birds is of any use to us. We are
Overtaken by fishing smacks, gondolas, and sometimes
A chip off a dream-heavy marble gets in (through
Its beauty, where I am most vulnerable) my eye.

I am always reading in the papers about the cold
And what will come of it, about crackpots, corpses,
About market forces, murders, and of a myriad
Ice-floes — but find little there to amuse me.
Why is that? I slam the door in the face
Of a beggar who comes at lunch-time, because
It's peace-time and one may spare oneself the sight —
Though not of the leaves, their joyless death by water.

Let us go on a tour. Let us sit under
Cypresses or under palms or in orange groves
And watch at specially reduced prices
Sunsets whose like has never been witnessed. Let us
Forget those unanswered letters to the past.
Time can work miracles. Though with debt battering
It comes at a bad time. We're not at home. In my heart's
Basement, unable to sleep, I find myself again
On chaff of derision, enduring time's autumn manoeuvres.

Geese

The in-formation
technology
of geese

can hear on its
high white
cirrus fibres

when the cold
is coming. Long
distance calls

awaken me each
morning. I lift
my head and let

the programmed
weatherline
croak on, watching

slack coils
of wire
stretch until

the message is
communicated,
then nestle

back to snore
snugly like
a warm receiver.

The Phoneless

Coming out of the subway, we saw them:
Different, and their lap-tops no longer
Held like the bows of front-desk violins
Poised to perform the opening of the Ring,
But attached to them as a beggar is
To his rattling Coke can. As if they had
For hours been lost amid the hiss and coil
Of an unspooling world serpent, restrained
Until now by sheer weight of endlessly
Linked voices, voices. Or they were escaping
Some terrible regression, up silver scales
And into the black of day.
                              Yesterday,
All the phones in three states failed.
                                    Computers
Designed to cushion consumers against
This sort of thing, to bypass overloads,
Overloaded, their rabid blathering spread
To systems in the neighbourhood, and soon
Silence was falling on D.C., Maryland,
Virginia, West Virginia, the maiden
Purity of peace: only that buzz-buzz
Cicada in the gingkos, where the wires
Futilely loop between telegraph poles —
Petrified tree-trunks on display outside
The Museum of Natural History.

Washington D.C., June 1991

Natural History

Like all the others here, my daughter,
My wife, and I are looking for
The Hope Diamond. A shuffling

Sunday of similar noses, up
Against 'cat's eye', 'adventurine',
Glossed but improbable names

By which to distinguish the real thing.
I, however, am distracted by a globe
On the farther side, displayed

Most plainly, the plain crystal
Ball of myth and fairy-tale —
Apparently, the world's largest.

I watch it, using television skills,
For some unconscious, prophetic shape,
But see, of course, nothing. Not even

Myself, only a risky feeling.
My family, meanwhile, have identified
The famous thing, which is blue

And cut by convention to a distant
Cold adornment. Unmoving,
But for the ill wind that stirs

Legend — how that millionairess,
Fearing for her child and for her stone,
Kept both under armed guard, till

One slips out with a delivery van
And is killed on the road. We separate.
The two I love entering a dark

Gallery of phalloids, snatches
From Fingal's cave, meteorite
Droppings, moon-rock; I, to look

Again into that crystal, never
Cut, but lovingly, secretively
Polished through months' and years'

Desire... Go, family, drifting on
Where the glass-eyed beasts gaze
Out through glass from a seamless

Artifice of property and paint —
The endangered, the extinct — and await me
Where you see a horned *Triceratops*.

Katie in a Prospect of D.C.

Outside the Oval Office,
My daughter started
To sing Humpty Dumpty.

Then, at a rising black wall
That dropped to a V,
She stopped singing and cried

For a flag of stars
To wave past the dark
Windows of the Space Museum.

On Capitol Hill, she
Chattered towards a life-
Size image of Jesus,

Was silent before the statue
Of the Father of Television,
Heard the floor whisper.

But approaching Watergate,
She pressed her investigative nose
To the glass, and broke in

On our conversations again
And again to report
What all the king's men couldn't.

Rosie in a Retrospect of D.C.

This little toon
That giggles from the depths
Of her sleep, flicking
Muscles in dream joy

Was less than a cel
Until we came
To Washington in a hot
June three years ago

To catch up with the Air
And Space and touch
Moon-rock and stand
Beneath that battered

Myth of Apollo,
Visiting all monuments
To the word shot —
And it was hot

Where she was conceived,
While the pumpkins
Flowered in the dry yard
And the cicadas

Wound their reels in
From the night, and we
Were hooked on the
Little Mermaid video.

To Maiden Castle

For my mother

When your father, to avoid another scene,
Took up his black box, left, and climbed alone
To Maiden Castle, all he was hoping for
Was peace. It was the late thirties: a Spitfire
Being test-flown overhead; along the lane,
The telegraph wires making siren sounds.
He wanted to see for himself, he said,
What the archaeologists were up to.
But you knew what he meant. The primal law
Of human nature: that relationships
Deteriorate, some in fury, some
To a cold war. What is it begins the end?
A mean squabble over a missing brooch,
A dropped ornament? Or your father's books,
Those books your mother detested so much
That when he died (*dust-gatherers!* she said)
She threw them out... Was it the books that day?
All those black words!
                                        It wasn't history
That drew him to the Iron Age hill-fort,
But musk of an exeat; the licence
To imagine, responsibility
Shelved, to look, to photograph, and instead
Of sitting long hours at his work scouring
Dry lines of a dull proof, to feel the ramparts
Break like a Pacific comber against him,
And capture in a light-sensitive frame
The moment.

He would have seen the trenches.
How the brigades floundered. Sir Mortimer
Smiling at his skeletons, their scooped-out
Neolithic skulls. He must have known too
The barrages. The arsenals. Fragments
Of a Venus. Offerings to the bull-god
In a thatched temple of Wisdom. Known them,
But never spoken of them. History
Was cinema flak.
                    It was the moment's beams
That he felt sway across and canopy
His threatened mind, its quiet interiors,
Its private spaces, clearing them of all
But present sensation.
                    And only this —
The photograph that he took — still survives
To help you piece his life back together,
As one might, from a brooch or an ornament,
Imagine the faintest outline of a race
Long vanished, their homes, their preoccupations,
Though never the words, the words that spark as
The ornament falls, the brooch goes missing,
Or a book is tossed resentfully aside.

Pass

The mist lifted enough for us to enter
Hardknott Pass. The notice beyond the sheep
Warned it was not to be tried in winter:
Single-track, hair-pin bended, and as steep

As 1 in 3. Into our sight come clear
Blue visions, then cataracts, and grey clouds
Stoop towards the rocks. But safe in low gear,
My parents seemed happier — there were crowds

Doing the same, after all. Wind down the glass
And span with a haiku that narrow space
Between styles. All images in this pass
Translate to our secure iambic pace.

And only when unchildlocked for the cairn's
Plunging view down to the walls of Hardknott Fort,
Where legionaries patrolled a high square
Nailed shut against all exultant thought,

Did we glimpse a map laid out — and my mother
A girlhood path that she and best friend Pearl...
Lost since the war, now somewhere in another
World, South Africa she thinks... The road's curl

A black ribbon untwining from a love
Journal. My mother clammed up. My father
Provoking her to *climb down the rest of*
The pass on your own now then, if you'd rather.

At the Eleventh Hour

For Daniel Hanvey, born 11th November 1993

Born into remembrance. While we observed
Two minutes' silence — you made the Great Push
From No-man's-land. While pensioners, unnerved
Three-quarters of a century, stood crushed —
You cried in triumph. While some who had served
Were named as breathing mist in the brief hush —
You made your landing on a spit of peace
Thrown up by war, and said that pain should cease.

You are for the next hundred years, not ours.
And though we all go over the top at once,
There will be those who ask: where are the flowers
That used to vein the fields from here to France?
And those who plough on, senseless as the powers
Instructing them, and make their blind advance
In one huge combine harvester, where youth
Is reaped and at the same time threshed from truth.

Of all their silos yield, of all their mill
Grinds to flour, remember this crumb: that we,
Whom Alzheimer's or a shot of morphine will
Have wiped clean of our unstaunched century,
We puffed at its dandelion clock until
We dreamt a flower our children's time might see.
So, little rootball of your parents' genes,
Take stock, and shoot, and show what Daniel means.

Barrow

Our brittle bones were chilled to envy
Even of the bones in Stoney Littleton
Long Barrow, where I had tapped

At a tubercular farmhouse to beg
And stood awaiting something at the entrance
To a chamber, sealed and on the list

For surgery. But there was no key.
And since our torch was not charged up, we
Gazed down a narrow beam of darkness

Imagining ourselves through there, to turn
And find this glow, as — looking back —
One might spot brilliance in a dark age.

Across the valley, the sun quite lost
In a serge-grey labyrinth, a whole field
Once filled with hay is landfill now:

Yellow skips, black plastic, keening
White gulls, and us — powerless
Above our age's burial mound.

An Offering

We live on the dry surface,
Power our grass short
And play over rich topsoil.
Keep a cap on the old wells,

Afraid to imagine what might echo
Under familiar place-names, or what
If we should stop turning
And pull, and lift the concrete.

My offering to the guardians
Of the thousand covered wells
Lost to mucilage, or filled
With hardcore and paved, my gift

To St. Anne, to Black Annis,
To you nymphs and water deities,
To all trout, snakes, toads, flies
That guard them still, is these

Lines that are bent like steel
Wishing pins — catch them! — words
Spin-gleaming through your legendry,
New-coined; and if you have no wish

For this severed head that sings
Its vaporous red trail
Down into your nursery rhymeless
Black, toss it back.

Behind Doors

I. NIGHTFLIGHTS

Then (the Mauls say) the only airport here
Was Heston, where Mr Chamberlain took off
For Munich. They had heard the peaceful cough
Of his pistons from their greenhouse, whose bleared
Panes crack with Boeings now so I can't hear
Their words about the war, but see the rough
Remains of their shelter and the stone cover
To their well, and wish... But my parents' fear
Permits me only to dream of those unseen
Dark places. Nightflights wink into the west
Across our hawthorn hedge, towards a Heath
Silence has stamped out like something obscene.
I go to bed, and with a tightening chest
Lie there, wait, listen, and invent a myth.

II. MIDDLE C

Those piano keys are keys to the doors
You never opened. When, in my innocence,
I bought you Mussorgsky's *Pictures,* and force-
Marched you through The Great Gate, you had the sense
To prefer a Promenade... but, of course,
That's you, to walk the self-effacing way.
Remember Middle C? The girl who looks
Down for a keyhole to help her; then one day
She's climbing up to 'perform' (your wry laugh!)
And finds that grand pianos don't have locks.
A moral, yes — but Mum, not even with half
A smile quote me that church bill *(THE MIDDLE ROAD —
THE ROAD TO FAILURE)* and say, 'My epitaph'.
You only followed the way the music flowed.

III. A POSTCARD TO STUART HENSON

Dear Stuart: rain's still streaming down the glass,
And once again we've not been able to get out...
A day at the dinner table then, door shut,
Grandma asleep. Blue willow-pattern vases,
Blue willow-pattern plates. Time passes
And nothing is on the page. I begin to doubt
My own abilities — but one can't spout
Poetry like rain, you'd tell me. One must cast
Gently into the stream, into that blue, fast-
Flowing moment when the mind is in spate;
Lean quietly on the Chinese bridge; and wait
For the line to quiver, the reel to at last
Unwind, wrestling with — unable to see —
This silvery form, a sonnet (from JDG).

Moving

For Jane

Rooks like dust in a home
Movie spatter the view
Through the picture window
As we peck at belongings
In your grandmother's bungalow,
Vacated now, up for sale.
The Natural History of Selbourne,
An Egyptian tea-towel,
Rusting weights and scales...
What can we do with this
Cracked windmill? that springless
Cuckoo clock? Now that she's
Bent into the storm-force
Of her ninety-fifth year,
Does she need this Shakespeare?

A gull outside peels like
A dressing where the barbed wire
Was surgically removed
And the poppies trampled
By the intruders who came
Deep in a summer's night.
Below that slope they parked
Invisibly and loaded into their van
Things that you do not see today.
There is no escape mechanism
Ticking in the hall now.
No willow-pattern blue
To glaze the emptied rooms.
Only detritus, only utility.
Only the rooks calling for more.

Beside the Wye

For Stephen Hanvey, 26th July 1989

Before we pitched, we went to the farmer's wife,
Who showed us the communal tap, and told us
That last Friday looking down from their patio
Over that bend where the lean young sallows
Meet the shallows on the smiling pebbly edge
Of a slow, grey and treacherous middle age,

Two youths appeared: the one to teach
The other to swim, to encourage him down
Deep into the Wye to where a sudden depth
Stirs then strikes and it's simpler to drown
Than wave, where the frogman who pulled up
The news said twenty-five feet. We filled up,

Then camped between two maturing ash-trees,
Swam naked out of sight of the farmer's wife,
Returning to our own fields, psychology, poetry,
The last load from Hay. I admire how you can dive
Into dreams, catch what softness nibbles the flesh.
Wonder, were those archetypes we both heard splash

As we trod the littoral? Think, I should look at
Modern Man in Search of a Soul, and try...
But now you talk of a camp-fire, ignoring this tinder
Among the loosestrife, bleached driftwood, dry
And light as balsa; and bring, like sacred ewes,
One on each shoulder, ash-logs that we instead use

As seats up here in this sedge confessional
Where the spark takes without any match, without
Need for old jokes about age, as if the years when

You aimed at a penny and missed, when I shot
And won atrophy, had never come between us.
The ash-trees are Masai listening for hyenas:

We talk through them, through tonight's Prom
Which comes from a palmy distant shell full of glees —
Bravo! Heave-ho! Ping-pong!   Talk of Hong Kong
Where you have lived... Of the boat people, refugees
Whom I knew... A hot-air balloon, almost the shape
Of misery, hangs; till a Phantom gives it a wipe.

We are out of sight of the river, of its ghosts,
Yet know we are caught within the coils of a World
Serpent meander, and as you send me now to Jung's
'Wotan', the storm that by dusk will have hurled
Day down from the nineties is crossing Offa's Dyke,
Bleating upon the Black Mountain, soon like

A crow to descend in low corkscrews. Two herons
Appear from the sallies to inform us the river
Is rising. The radio croaks John Major. The wind
Swings from the ash-top on a rope ladder whoever
Has the courage must climb. We drain red wine, our
Reunion bottle, before the peace turns to minor.

Satellite

A dish points outwards from our outside wall
To what we cannot see: stars that know all
More clearly than these nightly Movie Greats
The fate of earthen empires. The new estates
That blinker us from crystal ballroom spaces,
Haul us on in their fibre-optic traces,
Plough constellations; with a flash of shares
U-turning, leave the Great and Little Bears
Extinct, and gilt-edged bars of progress furrowed
Down the land's face. All that we have is borrowed:
Museums full of stuffed trophies slowly
Decaying. Territories that tick. Holy
Marbles seeming to breathe. Even these words I
Mix to purity, and this island time
We live on, living off serials, then soap,
And lastly just news — that shooting green hope
Our parents plotted as the world turned red,
Not with sunset, nor shame, but foreign dead.
We wait, hungry, now we have cleaned the Great
From Britain, scraped it out, shrunk it, wait
For a force beyond this uttermost storey
Of our high rise, a column whose glory
Will be to have relieved us of our fame,
Of all that mafficking, cheering of a name
Picked blind from a skull and nailed to the sky.
The dish receives its message from on high
In beams that swaddle the earth; in curves
Of parabolic reckoning. Then serves
Us word made flesh: chained bare Salome sprawled
Before us; while Civilisation's bald
Chronicler slots between those repeats of Wars
For King and Country networked in the stars.

A Pensioner addresses
the late Robert Maxwell

The mirror
could not show such greed:
your choppy style
left little sea-room for reflection.
And what need,
now you had made your pile,
but keep your dragon manners for protection?

The error
was that we grew old:
our wrinkly calm
left too much of ourselves invested.
We lost hold
and fell into your charm
and found the charming waters shark-infested.

The horror
when they knew you gone
and saw this boat
left no doubt where their thoughts were sinking:
old men drown,
but greed can stay afloat
to be washed up on a headline, green and stinking.

Seven Sea Interludes

I

Childhood is soft chalk: it allows the sea
To erode, almost to break through; were we
Forever children, there would be no Midlands,
Only sea air, a mirror-line of headlands.

II

Adolescence arrived like a storm beach
Overnight, with bodies, much sea-wrack, and each
Shingled face turning guiltily from salt
Ejaculations to identify a fault.

III

Student days hang like a pantomime horseshoe:
That bay on whose shores we held our barbecue-
Debate-cum-dance, loving the tides' motion;
Aware, of course, from lectures, of the pollution.

IV

As young couples we kiss to the cliff's edge,
Lie down with razorbills on a narrow ledge,
Laugh at the lifeguard, laugh at the fishing folk
In their corky craft, the sea is a huge joke.

V

Executive schedules seldom cover
The seaside; only if there's a lover
Or a business conference. One buys a yacht.
One moors it in Poole Harbour. The strakes rot.

VI

Parenthood is a final glimpse of the gold
You found on the beach as a one-year-old.
Return to the Landslip: the past gives way
And you are your children, have feet of clay.

VII

A Saga Holiday, perhaps. Promenades
Before supper, an evening playing cards.
Images in a land-locked single room
Of crossing the bar; stacks, arches; the blown spume.

Start Point at Day's End

For her, everything blows fresh, whether
It's a dull sea mist, the days a no-through
Tunnel of grey and rain and megalith

Seas forecast; or whether we all melt
Like wax effigies in the prickly spells
Of July. Whatever, for her mother and me

There was a staleness until this crisp light
And breeze came with late afternoon. Tension
Unfolding in little receding wrinkles.

Seagulls sit on benches outside the pub.
No shrieking, not even that hubble of
The machine that pays out pebbles, as a

Barmaid, beautiful sea-witch or mermaid,
Emerges from the weed and smoke to bring us
Foaming bitters and coffee like oil.

A small smack here at anchor makes
The sound of one hand clapping. Another
Is laying pots like peacetime mines.

Motors that have tightened garottes around
Bolt Head have been unchained, escorted
Back to lock-ups, their accomplices left

To dry out on the shingle. On the cliffs
One sober walker has walked into a cloud
Of red that he tells himself are moths

Hatched for sunset. No sunset yet: though
The tide is far out, and the Start Point keeper
Believes — poised, white — it's high time,

So pushes this evening our three-year-old
Swings on, high above the foreshore, towards
A half moon that's half-come, or half-gone.

Building the Boat

From holt and weald they drag
Extinct pines to be our keel,
While someone chips a flint.

From the New Forest they roll
Oaks to be carved to inflected
Norman ribs, while someone

Is melting copper with tin.
The Greeks give us olive pegs.
The Roman inspectorate moves in

To mark our water-line. And all
Is caulked with the bees-wax
From a dissolved distant priory.

On the prow is a plaque of laurel
With our dates and a painted eye
In green acrylic. Safely below,

And rigged in Egyptian white linen,
A Californian Big Tree someone
Has forged a way of holding in irons.

But our oars are of Norse ash: heave now
Towards the Black Sea whose huge waves
Rear, long over and not yet.

Huntingdonshire Eclogues

There is a property in the horizon which no man has but he whose eye can integrate all the parts.

Ralph Waldo Emerson

But it starts here.
A song about what is near.

Tomas Tranströmer

I

Here it begins, with the rains of December
that emboss our new north-facing panes and play tom-tom
on the polythene skin across our porch footings.

Like a breath of the primeval: savagely alone,
confronting the spray from Kinder Downfall, or
New Year's Eve paralytic among the Trafalgar Square

fountains ... Just negative ions, I suppose, making
the stone lions whimper in the subterranean passageways
of my past. 'Past!', our broken guttering echoes.

The water table must have been steadily rising all today —
a thought as cold as quicksilver threading a glass capillary.
The earth mother has lowered her pendulous warm front,

to lean so close above the bed where her water babies lie
that we may be cut off by our own daughter's bed-time.
Darkness is rolling in and the builders have all gone home.

They built the house across the lane on the site of a pond,
our neighbour tells us, and laughs at the thought that one day
it will inseminate that city couple's barren double brick ...

Behind them, a single field of darkness stretches hedgelessly
towards the Great Ouse. Our 'common stream', as brown
as a common hare, hides in its form there. It has been known

to close the A45. No traffic down the lane tonight,
except a pig-farmer's tractor trundling autumn slurry
away to spread, great wheels scattering pearls of muck.

II

The soil is just solid clay. I watched a man
outside the Bedford do-it-yourself store turning a wedge
left by the developers, and he looked like a

lone yachtsman ruddering the Atlantic — tarry
crests clung to his spade, his soles, and would not
grant him a moment's leisure. I have attempted

to walk some of the rights of way, have followed them
beyond the public footpointers, tracking their red
dotted tails to earth; but soon my legs felt as heavy

as a dismounted Crusader ... After the long rains,
a short stroll between the barbed-wire fences of a barley-field
can be like a spell on the Somme; and if you meet the ploughs,

they are Wellsian war machines, scarifying the landscape
to a nitrogen cloud. I always keep my head down
and search for little artefacts of peace, but have only ever

found pitiful fragments of a willow-pattern tea-set
between the JCB-smashed concrete chunks of runway
where Americans set out on their bombing raids. My neighbour,

born into an expendable shire, into a house
long drowned beneath a reservoir, has a collection of
black discs picked from behind his plough-team. Their jingle

is more of a bony click.   He lacks the cash it would take
to build a downstairs extension for his wife with her bad hips:
Wouldn't need no foundations, of course. That's solid clay.

The sky promises peaks that this landscape cannot offer,
so I have set out to reach the Folly, in the dream that
some climactic shaft may in a moment gasp between pink

lips of cirrocumulus and contour. To push through
rolls of clay is to conjure back those hours (it was a day
of unusual brightness) when I knew nothing but a square

of daylight glazing the birth-suite window, and Katie
pushing, pushing to be born. From the Folly there is a view
of the castle where Katherine of Aragon was at last confined

because she could not produce a son. But I am too late
to catch the crimson cortège shadowing the sequoia trees:
a darkness has stolen on to the scene, and my path

strayed to a thin palisade of elms whose bareness
is unlike the bareness of any other copse — a stripped
defensive circle in the middle of this prairie; a last stand;

an image of nature unswayed — did it not also broadcast
seeds of utter abandonment. Things blackly slither
and drop into its black pool at my approach. I do not linger.

There is a string of glass beads awaiting me on the A-road,
but first, I must turn into the breeze: that mature aroma
I tried to baby-wipe. In the field corner, on a heap of manure,

teats outwards, and legs splayed, pink as the sunless sky,
there is a sow: quite alone, fat, radiant, dead,
a smile on her face; and no pig-farm for half a mile.

IV

Three bare trees beside the castle. High up in their branches
you can see the mistletoe. I only noticed it on the last day
of term (the castle is a school now) when kids had stripped

off their striped blazers to hurl heavy sticks into the limes'
prehistoric bone-shaped silhouettes, and catch lucky sprigs
that they could use to squeeze a kiss from good-looking teachers.

I don't know if they got any: it grows so inaccessibly high,
only recognisable if you know to look for a skein of circuitry
poking out from a hole in lath and plaster. No doubt

male staff were all watching from the common room, some
thinking how they would have done the same
                                            had they been so young;
more wondering if they should shout to stop that foolery —

not because the mistletoe-hunt is a rite more wicked than
decorating a Christmas tree, or star-worship; but throwing
stones somebody might get blinded. They will find mistletoe.

And throw it at the history teacher who shouted at them
to stop it for their own good. But probably none of them —
since the only mythology they have been taught is medicine,

their only gods those white-robed elders who print out tales
of Cancer descending from the sun, Thrombosis
                                            arising from the waters —
none of them dare kiss, lest AIDS is unexpectedly delivered

to them this Christmas. I watched the kids frustrated beside
the bones of that heartless lime, beneath its out-of-reach
and sperm-filled berries. Baldr the beautiful is dead.

V

The well beyond our double-glazing is not from a garden centre,
nor a book of nursery rhymes: no gabled roof, no winch and pail
on a noose's length of nostalgia. Not a well you have to

throw dollar-bits into before you can draw up a dream. This well,
where we have imagined our new patio, is quite invisible, and capped
by stereo concrete slabs it would take Wagner's Fafner and Fasolt

to shift. A tub, a trellis, and a thick variegated mass
of creeping evergreen conceal it; and the larch-blade dividing our
property from our neighbour's (Jill to my Jack) bisects it.

In the Chilterns there is the Maharajah's triumphant Victorian bore.
In Derbyshire there are the summer carnival frames of clay and petal.
But this humble inbetween well is a memorial to a late absence

of mains water in Huntingdonshire, when the inhabitants of Stonely
and this row of terraced estate cottages (each one extended now,
each quite separate) came together every morning
                                        to receive their dark

benediction from the earth. How did they all live? I know one was
a gamekeeper who would hang his Sunday rabbit inside the well
to keep it fresh, while sixteen feet below him the unidentifiable

ancient coin glimmered enticingly. I have never looked into
this hole we own; but when Mr Corp, our builder,
                                        suggested we might
have to fill it in, his Welsh draughtsman brought a magic wand and,

as my wife held Katie back, the slabs slid clear for a moment:
a cool smooth-sided tunnel down through the years' alluvium,
through the clay left by the ice-sheets. She wished I had been there.

VI

Classes down to a third of their size, buzzing with tales
of abandoned juggernauts and cars in ditches. Is this what
we all secretly desire, to be simplified by an act of God?

Strangely, my colleague last night made the decision to commit
his thirties to the chaplaincy. This morning he got up and saw
a shroud over the garden and all roads from his village

blocked by what, it might almost seem, he had himself willed.
The car would only just start; and then that boyish slither
down Bustard Hill ... At school, our few kids read or write

about the snow, comparing the scene to the usual Christmas card.
He sees only that sealed white envelope. It is easy to write
your name in the snow and know that tomorrow or the day after

change will ensure it is erased — not so easy to sign away
the years. The cars pile up on Bustard Hill, and *Oh,*
they have killed a white bird up there ... I remember, Bram,

when you wanted to manufacture musical boxes
                                        — a means of escape:
you had one whose crisp Swiss mechanism played *Chariots of Fire.*
The thought of it upstairs perhaps helped warm that winter

of blank indecision. You didn't even go skiing, but sat brooding,
although you told me once you fear the day you are not fit enough
to run up a fire-escape and feel A1.   Locked in first gear,

you ice-axe the hill where the last bustard in England was shot.
Covington awaits you: its pub to be closed next Easter,
its church like a pewter chalice on a spread communion cloth.

VII

Poets live between their sheets of A4; but bricks are the thing
for ordinary mortals. Was it your great-grandfather, Stuart, lived
for a while in a 'Brickyard Cottage'? Now, having lain low

and watched the streetlamps creep closer and closer to your den,
you will do the same. Those stars you couldn't have borne to see
blanked out have guided you here where clay was cut and moulded.

Cover was all you wanted, and spotting across bare field rims
one small shabby copse and a house, you thought: a clean sheet.
Let those old mattresses, prams, abandoned fertilizer drums

stay hidden within the pit within the copse. 'Sign here!'
Your width-of-a-combine road whispered; and here — the arc-lights
of Molesworth on the horizon — you are.
                              HERE THE POET HENSON

LIVED FROM 1987- not, I'm sure, like another Sir Walter Scott
potboiling his life dry to pay for the bricks. Nor even a Yeats,
locked in that Tower, one skew-whiff ladder up to the arrow-slit.

But breathing pure John Clare; sweet verses of open air.
Nothing could confine such an image-maker; until the very
hedgerows became the walls of his asylum ...   Blue plaques?

Two peacocks were all that awaited us on the far side
of the ditch the day I helped you move in.   You have decided
to adopt them, feed them. And, since a Shell guide tells me

peacocks — according to Christian myth — are an assurance
of immortality, you were wise to christen yours so quickly:
Antony and Cleopatra! Perhaps Shakespeare was a peacock-lover.

VIII

March, and already the winds prove it. The Hunts Post tells me
the mad March hare can be seen in the open field these days,
boxing or lying low; but I have yet to see one. Wind

is all I have seen, or the effects of wind: one larchlap panel
in our fence had loosened and soon the boundary-line was snaking
wildly in the clay; so today a man has come with a steel rule.

The wind unnerves me. I cannot settle to anything; instead
of putting coherent words on the page, I find my eye is drawn to
movement in the lane: green fairy wands, and winsome ragged skirts

of my neighbour's weeping willow; or my ear is
                                        hooked on the squeaky
drag of insulated cable where it coils into my study and my Amstrad.
Then zephyrs from the window touch, like an Aeolian harp, that map

of the Stonely enclosures: each strip becomes a string that sounds
an aleatory life: *Mary Hemmings Lands, Jona. Cuthberts Lands,
Geo. Rusts Lands;* there *The Orchard,* here *Great Meadow,* and where

our garden ends, the inscription *Hare Close.* The thought of a hare
concealed in that post-war enlargement, in that blank exposure,
where two dozen families scraped an anonymous living, is as chilling

as today's wind. Hares were thought to be witches' moon-creatures,
symbols of increase and of long life; seek them in stone-age caves,
Egyptian tombs; they're as elusive as fire; the hieroglyphic hare says

Exist. It suits the hare that our hedges have gone, it leaves
his ballroom free: one sunrise you may glimpse two dozen waiting
in a solemn circle;   or at sunset hear one cry out like a child.

IX

A docket of yew into which my daughter plunges as we pass
because it's so dark, so inviting. A wicket, unhinged,
that leads to a webbed hammock swinging above a prickly

poisonous welcome mat. The neighbouring timber is sapless,
but incorruptible, and its fine memory scales down further even
than to childhood, Robin Hood, Little Red Riding Hood, to

the wolf. Behind this forest drop-scene stands a house where
once an unhappy family lived who have since left for a new start
in a young country where there are no muttering front-page yews

and where no toxin sweats them awake from feverish dreams
each morning, but all before them lies wide open and bright
as a Weetabix packet.   It was as if the brick

had framed windows that it did not want anyone to look into.
And then, one day, there was a police car parked outside
and rumours of a pack of hobnailed long-armed interlopers

digging up the garden ... He ran an antiques business.
Antiques such as every modern soul craves — we have the fairs
each Sunday and the rich come rolling so they can say they own

Grandma's brass bed-pan! The business had not done well
and the poor man took to hoodwinking. Next we knew, he was
doing a stretch; but the wife would take the dog out still,

smile merrily to those abiding within the law, before
darting back behind that defensive bank. You could almost hear
her tense smile snap like the released string of a long-bow.

In the fond illusion that this is a congenial habitat —
that we are permanent behind these neat vertical wall-stripes,
that we are utterly self-sufficient and (more to the point)

Heroes of the Great British Enlightenment, who lack no luxury
and will brook no wildernesses, but cut our lawns, and keep
the privet trimmed — we inhabit this temporary clearing.

To forget such thoughts, last weekend I took myself to Woburn:
but the path (Leisure Department's circular) skirted the game park —
buffalo on heat; rhino-horn at the wire; a quarantined jumbo

performing circus tricks, standing up
                                on an elm-stump to squirt — *I am*
free — more free than you in your forty-hour enclosure, you who fret,
pace and roar through your affairs, while I simply pirouette ...

Conditioned, of course; as we all are to watch *Wildlife on One*
instead of our own back doors where, for all we know, muntjac, black
squirrel, or unicorn come to copulate or to peer in at us glowing.

We only spot those nasty scratch-marks on the new
                                french window-panes
where panicky claws have attacked the glass; or the mouse-
droppings in our Habitat pine wardrobe; or on a July afternoon

thunderbugs that bite one and then die on one's clean shirt ...
These irritations are the sole brief contact with an impetus
that moves all about us; and momentary reminders of our isolation.

Blinded, clipped, hobbled, gelded, we gaze with calm indifference
past the terrestrial visitors on this Spring Bank Holiday:
everywhere the green eyes grow wider, willing us to *Look, look!*

He set crocuses and daffodils along Old Ford Lane
for others' pleasure. That we had noticed and admired them
pleased him immensely. As public, as rough-hewn, and original

as that concrete heart he laid before his sleepy wife one
St. Valentine's morning, and which still hangs beside the elm
stumps, impervious to disease. There was nobody else

we knew who would throw back their window and call from
dinner — *Have a claret!* — or *carrot* as I once misheard,
imagining some avuncular party-trick ... His generosity

was a magician's black box. One evening, we returned home
beneath a vast umbrella of fresh rhubarb: eaten, it set the date
for our daughter's birth! The day David Llewellin died

there had been unlooked-for perturbations in nature, the kind
bards exaggerate when a great man has fallen, the kind
Glendower boasted for his own nativity (*Signs have marked*

me extraordinary). When we tried, your last weekend,
to visit Spring Cottage, we found the skeletal footbridge
washed by a new ford; what had seemed a senescent trickle

become a lethal tide. By the time six days had carried
that week to its end, the waters had subsided, one willow
shattered, the rest of the lane swept grey. Now, today

as I push our daughter across your bridge, the Kym lies
peacefully retired; and in the uncut verges, crocuses
give way to daffodils, St. Valentine to Persephone.

Leaving the garden centre, I find myself tugged towards the river
by an invisible line. Struck by its cool unruffled progress
in spite of the thick electric air of this April afternoon,

and following the path — across a lock, beside a fresh willow
plantation, away from the cars and fancy barges for hire —
I thought of you, Chris, whom this landscape could never quite

inspire: your attempts to capture it were always like today's
grey thundery sky, something was choking to get out.
And I chastised you for not putting enough of the 1980's

into your art. Painting, like poetry, must contain news,
I pronounced. So when you unrolled the landscape east from here,
and you'd left in, like the shape of a missing penny stamp,

Barford Power Station, I would have approved, had a poet
born just below it, who thinks the works of Shakespeare and Rowe
more powerful than anything our high-tension age has strung,

not sung: *Paint water-meadows, paint the Golden Age!* Chris,
you've gone to another county now, to one more classical —
villas, august downs. On our prosaic by-pass, heavy

Laureates thunder towards their metropolis: my footpath leads
beneath such, through a mesh of hawthorn where high-voltage
lines converge: here I try to transform those cooling-towers

to what I had hoped you'd see: a huge and concrete henge
where mysteries that we have switched off for our palmy Spring
hibernate, and the Great Ouse curves knowingly past.

This morning's fierce debate (Mrs Thatcher and the Police State)
has calmed to thatched cottages and a faint aroma of pig ...
Our friends, who have battered themselves all year on the tubes

and against the bars of suburban London, have come here to recover
beneath these oaks. I walk them to the Stately Home and back;
but when our neighbour's trap comes clop-clopping through the mist,

they double-glaze: a clip from a Dickens film on *Breakfast Time*.
Nor will they believe that our newsagent closes today. I explain
you cannot change things too suddenly: he had those same blinds

down when a stray bomb blew news of the war on to the cobbles.
People like their Sundays left; their pram-resistant pavement
kept as it was; along with those ghetto-blasting church-bells;

even the Co-op has to dress up in Gothic script ... No, they will
never need the riot-shields in Kimbolton; Cynebald knew a safe seat
when he saw one! And what would anyone want to change? Except

those few who, in scattered yet-to-be-modernised cottages (usurped
horse-kings, forgotten drovers, pleachers of hawthorn, hollers
of clay), do without double-garages and swimming-pools ...
                                                This year two

such originals died: their names I never heard ... The developers',
the builders' names, the names on the cherished number-plates —
these I can't help but know. The lanes swarm with prospective buyers

out for a spin — seeds from a tough fast-growing urban species ...
Though all that ever seems to germinate is Leylandii: quick-
hedging that looks like the artificial grass they drape at burials.

Widescreen, to *Gone with the Wind* themes, the Spaldwick road
slow-pans you towards forgotten footage ... You spot the odd barn;
a token hawthorn butt; and countless anonymous farm-tracks —

but the tracks are too straight; harder than they need be.
Each barn, as you make your approach, becomes a corrugated hut.
The road unreels its title sequence but your senses are enmeshed

by the foulness of brussels, silage, or is it that dead hare
you swerved to avoid? You do not expect to find
                                                                          living things out here.
No house for miles, and apart from the bird-scarers, bird-noise

would be the only sound if you were to wind down the glass: peewits'
low-level, high-volume aerobatics; or the viffing of skylarks —
like two half-witted, crack-voiced veterans of the old hundred:

make a joyful noise unto the Lord of Air-space! And so it fell
that half a century ago Dwight Eisenhower sowed the bulldog's teeth.
But there was no Golden Fleece; only, somewhere over the rainbow,

the Rhein ablaze ... Now, occasionally, in the summer, a coachload
of balding shades will pause on its way
                                                        from the Madingley graves to hear
that this is the village where Clark Gable's suits were tailored

and none will be told the uncanny tale that the village keeps and
does not advertise: the local man who was up and out early jogging
the broken runways: who saw what he saw,
                                                        which is said to have been —

but secrets are what the Spaldwick road keeps best: the mist
encloses them more surely than the perimeter wire
                                                        seals Molesworth's lips.
Unnumbered aircrew must have left from here.
                                                        Some perhaps returned.

XV

A straight grassy track, broad as a road, yet not made up —
only for Delius lovers, Vaughan Williams drovers —
a bridleway which unzips the fantasy realms of rape, splits

the cereal boxes on the table-top, interrupts the unrolling
soap of everyday country farmside life, like a headline
that's truth and which can scarcely be believed amid so much

high yield fiction. I walk this straight grassy track trying
to ignore what surrounds me, the pollen-induced mirage
of fecundity that can find no need, so allows no room,

for skylark, hare's form, blue butterfly, or scattered poppies,
but will fuse in a core whole fields of sunflower, for
your breakfast. Dawn heightens Honeyhill Wood with its ad

glaze, the flattery of arc-lights: shooting has begun.
Not the gas-filled bird-scaring tube that I know to be bluff
and so pass at each field corner confidently, but shots

that smash clay, and send the black retrievers slavering.
Landrovers are parked and the colonels parade in camouflage,
pointing barrels towards the sky. This is a day of peace,

and this is what peace and prosperity entail: the rich,
unreal, utterly flat glory of a wide screen, which curves to
wrap around one's fears with illustrations of how lucky

we all are, forgetting occasionally to erase the odd
blemish from the past, such as this long green rural sentence
cut to such dips by four-wheel drivers that my foot slips.

On the main road I follow to work, there is a noise like wax
in the ears. You can hear it most clearly on a Sunday, when no
juggernauts are heading for their container shrine; but in winter

it swells the rush-hour; and on a Spring night it will make lovers
stir in their dark lay-by. I have visited the weirs at Offord Cluny
on a flood morning, and stood on the sluice-gates, and been stunned

by the sheer force in the hands of that one authority: a 125
crossing the crossing was all but drowned.
                                        And I watched the anglers,
silent, cowled like Cluniac monks; and a canoe and its paddle

hang cruciform in the race. But I did not imagine that our own
good brook (a dried-up ditch for much of the year) could ever abraid
such excitement. Yet today, out of interest, I left the right of way

and followed its sluggish course for the quarter of a mile or so
it meanders around to Hellett's butcher's shop. The cereal crop
pressed close to its banks; and there was brittle purpling elder,

ash-spears, scrawny umbellifer, and bath-brushes of teasel: enough
to put visitors off: the river all rags and bottles and bags; a geriatric
drugged asleep. Yet that gentle pumping sound, like the approach of

deafness, drew me round to a last bend and — yes — a secret weir,
walled and wheeled and with a swirling cochlea. How could I
not have walked here before? It would become
                                        a place of pilgrimage,

to bring poems and parents to; and perhaps even see a kingfisher.
Although to be honest, when a cloud passed
                                        and the vegetation shook,
it also seemed the perfect place to conceal some dreadful crime.

XVII

Where there is a space, they must always fill it
with an estate: this corner of the village was a rough
variety of meadows and hedgerowed paths. No use

to a soul, let alone an estate agent. So it is
to be sold, and fifty-seven 'dwellings' are to be crammed
between a meander of the Kym and the cemetery wall. Trees

must come down. And where those ponies now ponder and muse,
bulldozers will bray. Thus it is, was, and ever shall be.
That cottage, soon to be lost in rapid fugues of scaffolding,

is where the village organist lives. Then next door,
the Nonconformist chapel ... But that's already been converted,
a Fiat at the altar; and on the lawn, like a little fenced shrine,

someone's aviary, its flashes of a life overseas somehow
in tune with the notes inside me when I am moved to walk here.
Imagine them, all in black, that congregation of the Free Church,

trapped in its pews ... It would be a kind of justice if they
had become this song and bright ceaseless activity. But that
would be a foreign, unchristian fate for them. So now on down

past the White Horse. These days, I'm afraid, I drink more
than I offer up. What I truly worship lies outside, beyond those
pre-fabs (coming down soon for another estate): familiar greening

woodland in its slow curve towards a ripening Northamptonshire.
Hell would not be to have lived forty years with mice and draughts
in such a shack; but to be rehoused
                                where I could not see that view.

XVIII

Dancing on a dozen pin-sharp church spires, or swung out across
a high-voltage safety-net, Huntingdonshire's sky outshines
every one of its other acts. It is, after all, the only space

they can't infill. Its sketches for a Manhattan dreamscape
never get any further than the drawing-board, although the US
Air Force, we hear, has plans it's trying to push through:

our daughter shrieks at us — *SKY!* — and she could mean sparrow
or cruise-missile: all's one joy to her, she has inherited
her grandparents' war-steeped optimism. Retired to the north,

to the Peaks, my parents don't complain our Midlands are too flat,
or too fat, but smile rosily: *All that sky* ... although my father's
vision grows cloudy, and even with his silver-rimmed bi-focals,

newly prescribed, I know he would not find it easy to pick out those
far-off splinters of an ideal caught in theatrical striplight
where the stratus ends — Little Staughton, Pertenhall, and Keysoe —

spires which the youngsters, who come on Sundays bearing tripods
and spirit-levels, use as levelling rods to measure out and extend
their stake in the Home Counties. Fools' Gold, of course, but so is

the Siren-song of the Peaks. Today, discontented with the flatlands
and forgetting my parents' *be appreciative* smile,
                                        I beheld what some
would not find it worthwhile turning from a theodolite
                                        to witness: the sun

blitzing through to create a brief downstreaming gold-capped
pyramid of rays. Such an experience is over in a second or two, but
contentment rises in its silent bubble, and sounds the all-clear.

XIX

Ten miles: past gravel pits, along the crevassed verges
of the A604, and then through a maze of tiny agricultural tracks.
I hardly knew where I was going. I had no torch, no map.

Fidelity led me into this strange county, dizzied by ring-
roads, dazzled by oncoming juggernauts, hooted at by dark owls.
No moon, no stars. The signposts pre-war and unreadable. If a car

loomed on an uninhabited stretch, I would jump into the ditch,
too embarrassed to be caught, fox-guilty, in those 1 a.m.
headlamps. I had been away on an EFL course, and my wife

left to oversee our move into Huntingdonshire; that evening,
a killing silence on the phone: it was to do with desire, but
more with the need for conception. I sent flowers: the worst thing —

which only left me one last train, and no taxi-fare. Huntingdon
to Kimbolton on foot; the neon ghost-glow of rape, cash-crop grown
for the seed, not the flower; fatigued brain turning fat King Henry

on its spit, who picked our new home
                                as his first wife's prison, thought
he could put away love and let his lust roam. Overlooking that castle
where she pined, the bedroom where my own wife is a green haze.
                                                    I hurry

through fields in which no feelings can be hidden ...   Even today,
our housebound and telephoneless neighbours
                                seem to know about all the
separations and liaisons in Kimbolton.
                                Only this morning my wife took

flowers to thank them for babysitting, and she came back full of —
But then they probably also know how after that mad sleepwalk of
five years ago, I stood and threw gravel at her window, grovelling.

XX

I have walked to the Warren and found there a horseshoe,
and wondered if it was truly a relic of the team-ploughing,
or just one lost by a cantering school-girl looking

for bridleways: and I have held it briefly like a quoit
half despising my short-lived impulse (hang it up
to catch good luck!), half thrilled that I might be seeing

through its keyhole into an elm-trimmed whitethorn and
blacksmith Huntingdonshire, where our local farrier
hammered this same shoe fifty years ago, when my neighbour

unlettered, unhurried, would have been standing watching
the sparks peal from the forge, then have followed his huge
plough-horse out of the travus, over the field he had to till.

The field I cross to reach Warren Hill must have been
ten fields then: there's a machine with caterpillar treads
parked ready to eradicate these pocked strips of charred

stubble, burnt upon harvest. Respect for fire lives on —
the word in red illumination flashes as you slow down
and take the bend. Wieland is in hiding. There, where

mechanics work their deft magic on a Scandinavian combine,
and have hung one of their workshop's rusty horseshoes,
points to the earth; or in that tubular alarm calling

volunteers to out-of-control and wilful late summer
burnings: folk congregate, strangers pull over, as if
for a white wedding, and the air is specked with passion.

XXI

No Huntingdon White Horse, no feature carved by Grim
or dropped by the Devil, no Tor where Alfred or Arthur might
have sat, no headless pack of hounds, no Dragon —

but a solitary antlered figure that seems to have leapt
from a Palaeolithic cave wall in France, prancing
across the eastern English landscape like a hobby-horse,

to the steps of a dance that has even inspired the wind
to a composition, and which it has sketched in starlings
on the horizon: *Oss, oss, wee oss!* it sings to itself

at winter sunset. Or when the stubble-burning is in progress,
it crackles and strides between the dying fires like
a Druid wicker man. But on schoolday afternoons, it looks

a procession of bare facts through the classroom window:
the progress of power; Cromwell's Ironsides about to charge;
Queen Katherine's funeral cortège draping the county.

First dawn of the holidays I was out walking through
one of those islands of scrub kept solely for the game
and saw a sudden flash that I took to be Roe or Fallow,

but as I moved to where it had been, it became a skeleton,
man-made and erect. There is nothing at all ghostly about
a pylon — grey folded arms, the sheen of gun-metal — yet

home, I lit at once our little stag-headed altar:
the images flickered comfortingly as I lay chained by
my imagination, a landscape barbed with the literal.

XXII

First day in the lane our neighbour informed us: *You've had
a fox at the door. Thirty-five years I've lived in this row, and
never seen one come right up to the step like that!* More

the thing, I found out later, is a few dozen hounds on your lawn ...
You soon meet them, loitering with intent to cull — Heaven's Devils,
mods and rocking horses — blocking the yellow roads.
                                                    And that wave

they bestow, so derisive, so mechanical. *Our blessings upon you,
motorist!* You slink past. It's enough to make one turn saboteur.
Yet they have a scent I would not wish to lose; it leads us back

towards myth: pale horsemen, the demon pack. Whenever I hear
that far-off yelping, it is like something caged in
my own mind. I knew a young girl torn apart by the dream

of a fox, of being hunted by a fox; and there was another
whose brain was scattered in our village here, when something
outside the butcher's made her horse shy; but the hunt went on.

Foxes hop into their red getaway car, smiling a Mafiosa smile.
Last summer, the row seemed to be closing in. Fine before
the child came, now my study was a nursery: we would move.

So we drove out house-hunting. But as we spotted one in red brick,
a black London taxi-cab ignored a Give Way sign and then failed
to indicate. I could only do what my instinct barked — brake!

The taxi, black, all its windows black, sidled on without stopping.
And we did not move then or in the following months; but a fox
winked pointedly, looked right, looked left,
                                        and drew away up the road.

XXIII

When you take your car up to Catworth Filling Station, the man who
drives you back — blue overalls, white hair, and the hint
of a stammer — tells you that he used to drive a steam engine,

tells you as he glides you down the B660 (Catworth is way off the
bus routes) about the unrivalled beauty of the run up from Peterborough
to the Peaks, but also of his special love for the local Kimbolton-

Kettering line: he points out the station — your oiled and tuned
Austin singing over the stone bridge —
                                   a glimpse of clean washing hung
outside the waiting room, an aerial on the signal box. A busy

station until the line was closed: pulled up with the ease I press
CUT on this word processor and watch a sentence
                                        of Dickensian length,
plushly syntaxed, its etymologies, its allusions, peel into limbo.

Nothing of the old straight track can be walked — still either
BRITISH RAIL KEEP OFF, or wheatfields — but from the road its
stigmata cross the pale-skinned landscape, green and luxuriant

like the long barrow of a forgotten king. Once I committed
two crimes: first by trespassing there, and then by uprooting from
the trackside a runner of *Rosa canina* for our private reserve.

Planted, it soon submitted its own plan for a network: branch-lines
in profusion!   But the old man driving your freshly MOT'd Mini
A-reg does not mention names, and so you do not ask him about Lord

Beeching, but talk of elms, hedgerows, meadowland; and wonder
what he might make of the computer terminology you are learning,
drafted late as he was into the service
                             of the internal combustion engine.

XXIV

At Gimber's End, there's to be no more truck with sugar-beet.
Where a last few elms hang on, and the temporary sign
says SLOW, JCBs clear unprofitability into a bank

and scoop out a clay pit. Not, as it happens, a building site.
Nor a stable tomb in which to dispose of the sun-god. Merely
a reservoir, stocked with trout, trimmed with false bulrushes.

Sixteen steps lead up towards this new setting for the sun:
and when my daughter climbs ahead of me and her glance back
cries that there are wonderful things, two swans, like sentinels

come drifting across the evening. And as I watch them,
a female silhouette appears, with a white vessel, haloed
by strange light from the west, on which I'm convinced

she's about to remark; or perhaps a word to the child. Then I
will say how good to see some enrichment of our landscape,
that of all beauty's elements, water is the most precious ...

Private property's all I catch from the mouthful she flings
lugging her plastic swill-bucket up the steps. I flush
into the evening sky; and though I desire to keep the peace

by telling her that when I dug, coped with clay, the cost
of butyl, the span it might last before decay by sunlight,
how slowly it filled, how fast the fissiparous pond-life spread ...

Instead, I begin to defend the right of way we've followed —
How'd you like strangers cutting through your front garden? —
stumbling back down as the swans are fed waste and privatized.

XXV

September: we had been expecting the frosts to move in.
But today it was suddenly warm, and the sky a cerebral
ripple of stillness. I took Keats out to beat the bounds.

But we were prevented by a hand carrying a can half-
full of blackberries, by lips complaining that they aren't
plump like they used to be, men don't trim the hedges,

keep charge of the landscape like they used ... Sharpening,
this keen slow gaze reduced me to a grey scythe-stone;
pierced me with blue, a bitter blue, camouflaged in cheery

lengths of hedge-talk. He did not know me; he guessed
I must be a city-boy because I stood on the bend, one heel
kicking LONDON 63 MILES. He was born here — before the war,

before the First War. And as he talks, I feel myself
rolling on moss, and imagine this figure climbing the years
always between persistent green flares of elm, upright,

looking for ripe fruit. He points to where men have failed —
a trench neglected, some kind of outlet — and then at
the new half-timber home, winking — *Not had floods for a while —*

they won't know what hits them ... And then I told him,
dislodging the stone from my tongue, of old Mossie next door.
And the shift in his tanned smile was not so much shock

as a jerk to avoid another acorn. I did not open my small volume
after that, but walked the rutted clay around the back
of the village, past the allotments, towards the primary school.

XXVI

The autumn our daughter was conceived, I spent all my time
pocketing acorns. Ammunition, in part, to fight off
homogenisation of our landscape; a way of penetrating

the tractor-drivers' ear-enclosures; but I'd half thought
if I could deposit a few in some unsprayable wild patch
amongst the detritus of a pound — Victorian shares and stock

droppings — there might be a chance of their germinating.
The small oak I planted in our own front garden, to dull
our neighbours' gilt-edged flashily poisonous laburnums,

had a splendid crop, its first — but though my fingers itched,
I was foiled: a passer-by had asked if she could take them
for the *Blue Peter* tree appeal ... and since, there have been

no acorns. Only this child of ours: erasing all earlier plans,
stripping the days, to set about making of them a Pleasure Ground.
Instead of our sitting in front of *Gardener's World*, she will

drive us to Wimpole Hall to witness a dray-horse, touch a sheep ...
The Great Hurricane that, in the October of 'eighty-seven,
revolutionised the South-east and felled much mature oak,

wrecking an eighteenth-century Greening's sophisticated
complex of paths and prospects at Wimpole, had already hit
this Greening eighteen months before; my little oak held firm,

and still I had great plans — for all a pimply scarlet rash
rusted the leaves that Spring, for all the veneers of another
season's cup-and-ball game lay mouldering in my jeans pocket.

XXVII

I know nothing about birds — but I know that now we have put out
a table in the back garden, somehow they come, demanding that we
take down our guide and identify them. And even when they're not

at their bosomy, fish-net aerobics, their Siren voices bubble
like the bacchanalia from a winemaker's cupboard. I cannot divine
anything from that twitter; it is as meaningless to me as Messiaen.

Yet I know people who live in East Anglia just because of the birds:
a hide to them is a sight as mysterious and sacred as Stonehenge.
To these high priests of ornithoscopy, Grafham Water is not the

reservoir where of an autumn evening I have watched swans pivot
and dip on their perspex mounting like a first toy; or where
the whipping of an angler's line, or a yacht's tilt, has caught my eye;

but a lacustrine altar to which wild geese and waders flock; where if
some exotic visitor is expected, they will know, and you see them
raise black prismed glasses. I cannot share in their excitement

for such distant splashes; although occasionally, we have driven here
for an afternoon tea, and skimmed stones,
                                 and let Katie feed the ducks.
But ducks are all drakes to me; and every mallard is imaginaire.

What's actual is that afternoon when Jane had just left hospital:
we had left the little bundle with its great-grandmother, breathing
steadily towards a second week or ninetieth year, and come out

to get some air, to prove to ourselves that this had changed nothing.
But something made us suddenly turn back and, in a white flap, pump
madly home to check that she hadn't —
                            I don't know what — flown away?

XXVIII

Where the US Air Force besoms the summer from the trees,
with not even time for a child to wince in horror,
much less to crane round from its car-seat to see,

the roadside stall sells pumpkins: it is the highlight
of our trip back from swimming for her to identify, then try
to pronounce these Cinderella-flavour, Rumplestiltskin-

shaped morphemes. Today, Mummy has decided she will let
our hair down and buy one, scoop it out, to make
soup or American pie; and put a candle in the empty skull

for Halloween. Katie was asleep when this ribbed moon rose
and then set on to the white formica work-top opposite
the doll her Aunt Tode sent her from Haiti. I lowered it,

conscious of its mythological bulk; but it was as yet
entirely pumpkin — we had only to take the knife
to its skin, cut out the eyes, gash a grin ...

But still have not, although we keep a festive candle
for those odd epiphanies of no-power when we will sit
star-struck before curtainlessness, feeling

televised in our own home. At the last failure
I failed to locate the matchbox, and all I could see
was what I'd suppressed from my daylight thoughts: shots

of an old woman who drowned herself in our garden well
years back. Did they accuse her of something? The kids come
shrieking with their Massachussets roll: *Trick or Treat?*

XXIX

Bewitched is on the television; out at the back
a full moon rises over Town Hill. Katie is crying past
the screen, though not to the moon: *Cat! — Look!*

I can hear nothing through my moon-yellow headphones,
purring *Mainly for Pleasure* continuity. She tugs —
Daddy! Cat!, but I'm taken up by a heavenly skirl.

The day has been all gales; the branch of a Scots Pine
just missed me as I was walking home, but now our new birch,
silver for the first time since I put it in, becomes a slender

beam that can play this compact disc of night-music.
Day's shellac spin begins its slow glissade.
A whiskered shade picking the choicest bits of our refuse,

drags a St.Ivel carton up to her fence-post, which is loose.
She looks at me, and my daughter begs me to let her in.
But I will not miss this one last piece of magic, the moon

a hologram on the clouds, hurtling to utter obscurity,
Malcolm Arnold's *Scottish Dances* playing to the end.
The two of us await the re-appearance of a Mini between

the moon and the silver birch, where the rush-hour
brooms home from Felixstowe. The double-glazing turns
windows to mirrors as it darkens, until only my daughter,

nose pressed up against her own image, is visible.
Weighed down with Waitrose bags, you arrive, bringing a lamp
to keep from her new bedroom all this gloom and moonshine.

XXX

Our village alchemist, high priest, who crowned
the Queen's Silver Jubilee with ore of gold and set
Cleopatra's Needle in gems from his richest barge,

who rose through ecstasies to the top storey of
the Shell Building, and exchanged jokes with the Duke
and various Princesses; our famous gunpowder Reverend

today sent nothing up into the sky; although he did try
with the revised version of the Book of Common Prayer
to lead us through the Valley of the Shadow, but the words

fizzed and went out. Then nothing happened. Spectators
wandering away ... But we at last walked to where the cedar's
dark flames lick and spread, and there like an unexploded

ashbud he stood, glancing up into the wind, telling
the man with a spade that this was his first interment
in twenty-five years: all the others, he said, had been —

but here comes the cortège: only the wife, the son, one
remaining cousin of this oldest original inhabitant ...
Ploughman, it might have been said, worker for the duke, fire-

warden, school washer-up — as it might also have been said
he was content with his allotment, immaculate lawn, hedge,
had all words not been crushed by the bulldozers' *Little*

bit of meadow and no peace ... The coffin is lowered,
and an arm like a black turnstile moves them on to dazzle
at the vacant grass, at a few brief extravagant cascades.

XXXI

The shortest day. The day the sun stands still.
The builders have set their jingle and news mixers to grind:
We wish you a— (earthquake, aircrash) *Christmas Sale!*

It cannot stop, and there are few hours enough of peace
in this twenty-four. My wife is out last-minute shopping.
Our daughter is in her cot. An opportunity now

to celebrate the winter solstice in these heaped-up
prunings of the year, needing only the tranquil spark
to set words ablaze. O come, o come, imagination! Tonight

we are going out to play *Trivial Pursuit* — tomorrow
three men arrive to lay vinyl — and then it will be
all unwrapping and over-eating. The carol-singers knock,

the baby awakes: and screams. O let the sun stand still
and give me time to put a star to this six-month-old
bundle of image and phrase. My wife returns. Not speaking,

we unpack carrier bags; between us make a dolmen
of our silence, passing our daughter through it, sacrifice
to some Neolithic moment, set before we have even

spared it a shiver. I draw a giant sun, like a giant
yellow medieval mace, with a crayon. My wife makes
shadow animals in the late beams on the wall.

The shortest day is over, all its possibilities a
dim line on the horizon. The sun has begun to move
again; we sulk and strain to see through the fog.

After we'd been last night to look for the ghosts of ridge
and furrow on the snow-trimmed fields at the end of the lane,
The Winter Walk at Noon was my bed-time reading.

This morning, the river that lay flat in the field's lap,
passive as Cowper's hare, has broken into a wild rush —
a rip hisses across the gravel track to Gimber's End.

My neighbour is out complaining about the lack of ditches:
It's the council. These bloody houses. I don't care —
they can put up many as they want now! And stiffly,

futilely, sweeps the waters from his gate. Strangers
are stopping to watch the pageant: the country's new regime.
Why did nobody predict that this sorceress would arise?

Range Rovers glide across the surface. Estate and Saloon
approach: bald heads in their glass islands pray.
Minis turn back to St.Neots, to the saint of all Minis.

Noon is bright with the spirit of river nymphs:
the smallest hill looks the pap of a goddess. Reasonable
William Cowper keeps dropping words into my head as if to

dam these pagan emotions. *God made the country!* — but
my neighbour, who is dour and flat-voiced, replies
It's more like a town, these days ...   *The Independent* arrives,

and on the front page is a Huntingdonshire tragedy: a mother
dives to snatch her toddler from the floods, and drowns. The father
tries to rescue her; he also drowns. Only the child crawls out.